World Deserts

Reader

Core Knowledge®

Copyright © 2018 Core Knowledge Foundation
www.coreknowledge.org

All Rights Reserved.

Core Knowledge®, Core Knowledge Curriculum Series™,
Core Knowledge History and Geography™ and CKHG™
are trademarks of the Core Knowledge Foundation.

Trademarks and trade names are shown in this book
strictly for illustrative and educational purposes and are
the property of their respective owners. References herein
should not be regarded as affecting the validity of said
trademarks and trade names.

ISBN: 978-1-68380-318-8

World Deserts

Table of Contents

World Deserts
Reader
Core Knowledge History and Geography™

Chapter 1
What Is a Desert?

Desert Landscapes When you hear the word *desert*, do you think of a hot, dry place where nothing grows and everything is covered by sand? Some deserts fit this description, but you might be surprised to learn that not all deserts are sandy or completely barren or even hot. For example, there are **polar** deserts in the Arctic and in the Antarctic region.

The Big Question

What features determine whether an area of land is a desert?

Vocabulary

polar, adj. relating to a geographic pole or the area around it

The Sahara is the largest nonpolar desert in the world.

Most **climatologists** define the word *desert* as a place where **evaporation** exceeds **precipitation**. One feature of a desert can be its dryness, or aridity. One way of assessing the dryness of a place is by measuring how many inches of precipitation it gets in an average year. Most deserts get less than ten inches of precipitation a year—this is also true of the Arctic and the Antarctic region. Compare that meager ten inches with the average yearly precipitation in some major American cities:

City	Average Yearly Precipitation
New Orleans	61 inches
New York City	42 inches
Chicago	35 inches
Dallas	29 inches
San Francisco	20 inches
Los Angeles	15 inches

Vocabulary

climatologist, n. a scientist who studies weather patterns over time

evaporation, n. the process by which a liquid changes to a vapor or gas

precipitation, n. water falling to Earth's surface as rain, hail, snow, or sleet

The two largest deserts on Earth are the Antarctic Polar Desert and the Arctic Polar Desert. This image shows an area of the Antarctic Polar Desert.

Even when it does rain in a desert, plants and animals are often only able to use a small amount of the rainwater. For example, sudden thunderstorms can cause heavy rainfall, but the water quickly runs off in flash floods and does not soak into the ground. When a light shower falls over a dry desert area, most of the rain evaporates before it touches the ground because the air is so dry.

The strength of the sun is also a factor. When temperatures are very high, as they are in many deserts, evaporation speeds up. Because of this, the water has less time to soak into the parched soil.

Desert Temperatures

Many deserts are hot as well as dry. Not surprisingly, deserts near the equator are very hot. In the Sahara in Africa, daytime temperatures routinely soar well above 100° Fahrenheit (F). However, the highest recognized recorded temperature was measured on July 10, 1913, at Greenland Ranch in Death Valley, California. On that day, the temperature reached 134°F.

Deserts far from the equator tend not to have the scorching hot temperatures of the Sahara. In fact, during the winter, these deserts can be freezing cold. The average winter temperature in the Gobi in northern China is 10° to 15°F. And then there are the polar deserts. In the Arctic Polar Desert, the winter temperature can drop below -60°F.

One feature that both "hot" and "cold" deserts share is a dramatic change between daytime and nighttime temperatures. At night, the temperature in a hot desert can drop anywhere from 30° to 70°F. Clouds keep warm air near the ground. Desert skies, whether they are hot or dry, are often cloudless, so at night much of the heat rises into the sky, leaving the desert much colder than it is in the daytime.

Major Deserts of the World

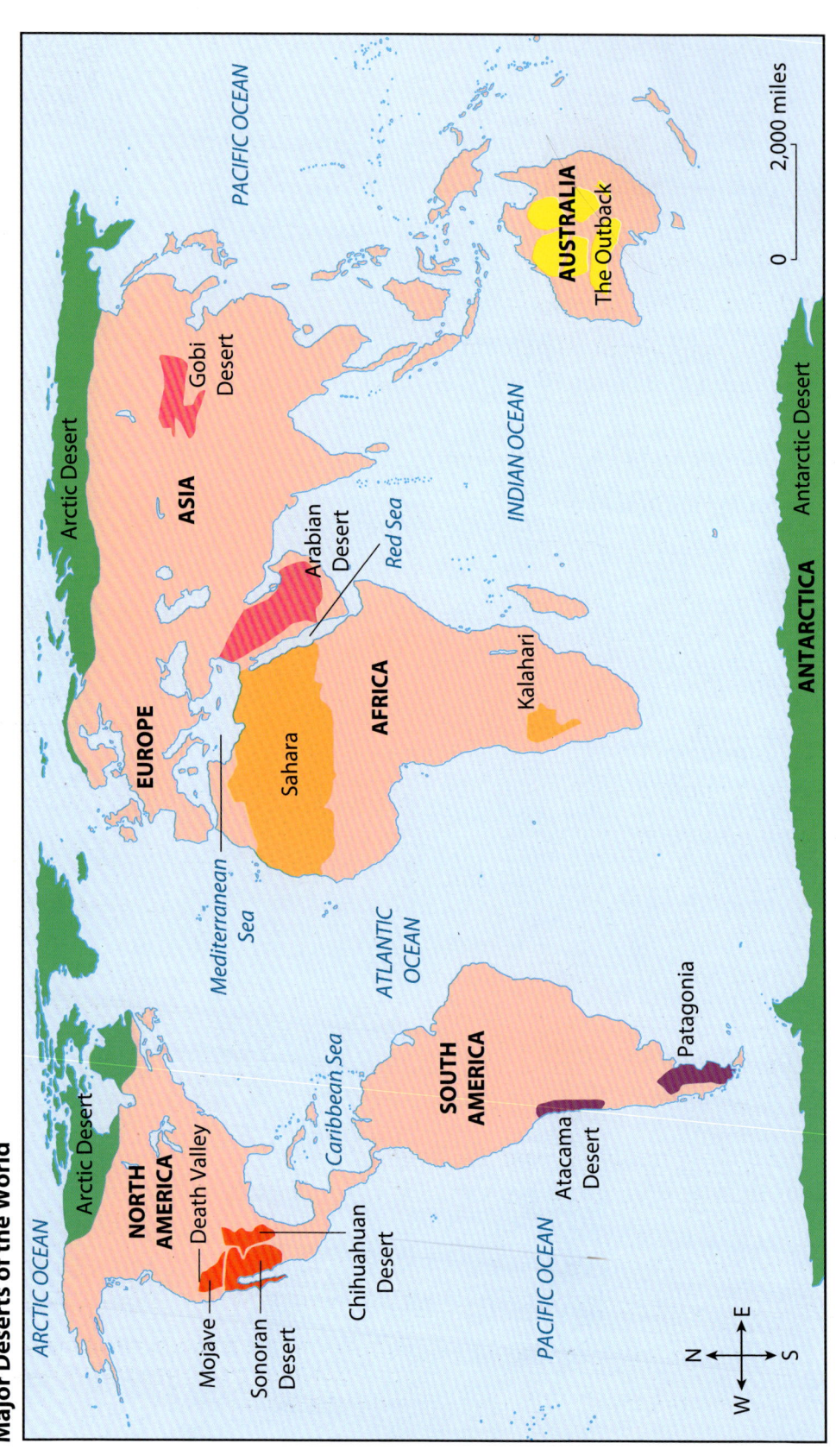

6

Desert Landforms

Some deserts contain great seas of sand, but other deserts have little or no sand. Only about 2 percent of North American deserts are covered with sand. The Sahara, famous for its sand dunes, is only about 10 percent sand covered.

Just as deserts can exhibit a wide range of temperatures, they can also contain many different types of landforms. Deserts can have mountains, plateaus, or plains. Some are covered with gravel, bare bedrock, or sand.

Sometimes the desert landscape is scarred and crisscrossed with ravines, gullies, and canyons caused by rushing water from flash floods. On those rare occasions when rain does fall, the water runs downhill, carving a path through the thin soil. Eventually the path turns into a ditch, the ditch into a gully, the gully into a ravine, and the ravine can even turn into a canyon.

Desert winds also shape the landscape. The wind blows away whatever thin topsoil there is, leaving behind sand, rock, or gravel.

Great Sand Dunes National Park, in southern Colorado, is known for its spectacular dunes.

Here you can see how over many, many years, water has worn away the landscape to create a ravine.

Life in the Desert

Although some deserts of the world can be difficult places to live, over thousands of years groups of people, as well as animals and plants, have found ways to survive. The key to survival is the ability to adapt to the environment.

The giant saguaro (/suh*war*oh/) cactus grows in the deserts of southern Arizona and northern Mexico. To survive in the desert, the cactus has adapted to the environment in several ways. Its stem is fleshy and thick, allowing it to store enormous amounts of water. It has no leaves that could lose moisture. It also spreads its roots in a wide area near the surface of the soil. This enables it to absorb, or take in, as much water as possible during the infrequent rains.

Camels live in the Sahara and in other deserts. They can go for long periods of time without drinking. The North American kangaroo rat is even more ideally adapted to desert life. It can survive its entire lifetime without sipping a drop of water.

Kangaroo rats get the water they need to survive by eating plants, such as cacti.

The giant saguaro cactus has adapted to life in the desert.

It gets moisture from seeds and plant leaves, which contain small amounts of water. However, its main adaptation is the special water recycling system in its own body.

The kangaroo rat's kidneys recycle water internally. The animal loses very little water through natural processes. When a kangaroo rat has to relieve itself, it leaves behind a patch of crystals instead of a stream of liquid urine.

Many desert animals, including rats, mice, squirrels, and lizards, are nocturnal. They avoid the harsh heat of the daytime by burrowing deep into the ground and coming out only at night.

People have also learned how to survive in desert areas. For example, some native peoples of the American Southwest learned how to use irrigation systems to water their crops. Entire Native American societies lived in American desert lands. This is also true of the history of groups of people who live, or once lived, in the great deserts of Africa and Asia.

Today, there are large cities in desert areas of the United States and across the globe. Lots of people have their homes in deserts. New technologies involving irrigation for crops, and dams for storing water, as well as access to deep wells underground, have made life in such environments perfectly possible. Areas of desert have quite literally been transformed into populated city centers.

Growing Deserts

Although desert areas may be shrinking in some parts of the world, they are growing in others. In parts of Africa, **desertification** is a major problem. African farmers in need of farmland have cleared and planted on **semiarid** lands near the edges of the Sahara. When farm animals nibble away the plants in these areas and farmers use the scattered

> ## Vocabulary
>
> **desertification,** n. natural or human processes that turn fertile land into a desert
>
> **semiarid,** adj. describing locations with little precipitation, but with enough moisture to support the growth of grasses, shrubs, and a few scattered trees

Las Vegas is a thriving, bustling city in Nevada's Mojave Desert. The average annual rainfall there is 9.63 inches.

brush for fuel, there is little or nothing left to hold back the winds. Often these winds blow away the thin topsoil and blow in desert sand.

Today, about 20 percent of the world is desert. Changes in weather patterns, together with changes in the ways people treat the land, will determine whether that number shrinks, grows, or stays the same.

Chapter 2
Deserts of Africa

The Sahara A caravan of camels makes its way across endless sand dunes. It follows a route between shifting dunes that sometimes rise several hundred feet high. The camels labor along at a steady two miles per hour. They each carry nearly four hundred pounds of salt from the salt mines in the desert.

The Big Question

What are the similarities and differences between the Sahara and Kalahari deserts?

A camel train crosses the sand dunes of the Sahara.

The heat is brutal. The sun is high overhead, and the sand is reflecting its heat. Fortunately, camels are designed for this kind of heat. Their long legs keep their bodies well above the burning sand, their stomachs hold a lot of water, and their humps contain fat that can be used for energy when food supplies are short. But the humps have begun to sag, a sign the camels have gone too long without food.

The caravan leaders are not worried. They know that just over the horizon is an **oasis**, where they and their animals can rest in the shade and replenish their food and water supplies. The camels can each drink as much as twenty-five gallons of water, and their humps will firm up when they graze at the oasis. The food and water they take in at the oasis will be enough to last for about a week.

For thousands of years, camel caravans have carried goods across the Sahara. Even today, camel caravans go to remote places in the Sahara that trucks cannot reach.

Vocabulary

oasis, n. an area in the desert where there are plants and water

Oasis in the Sahara

The Sahara is a patchwork desert of rocky mountains, **salt flats**, gravel plains, and sand seas. It stretches about three thousand miles across Africa, from the Atlantic Ocean in the west to the Red Sea in the east. It is 1,200 miles from north to south and covers three and a half million square miles. That's almost the size of the United States.

Fennec fox

Daytime temperatures in the summer are extremely hot. But like most deserts, the Sahara does not hold the daytime heat. Nighttime temperatures can sometimes drop to freezing during the cooler months of the year.

The Sahara is drier than most deserts, with an average rainfall of less than four inches per year. There are many years in which no rain falls in some parts of the desert. Nevertheless, the Sahara does have widely scattered permanent water sources, such as oases. And the world's longest river, the Nile, runs through the eastern part of this largest-of-all deserts.

Despite its barren features, much of the Sahara supports a variety of plant and animal life. Many plants have special root systems that reach deep into the earth to find water. Both large and small animals live in the Sahara. There are antelopes that rarely drink water but that get their moisture from the shrubs they eat. Gazelles and wild mountain sheep roam the dusty Sahara. The small fennec fox, whose large ears **radiate** heat from its body to help keep it cool, also calls the Sahara its home.

Vocabulary

salt flat, n. an area of land where evaporation has left a layer of salt

radiate, v. to send out

The Sahara supports human life too. Although fewer people live in the drier areas of the Sahara, millions and millions of people live on the desert margins.

Some parts of the Kalahari can support a large variety of wildlife. Here you can see lionesses resting during the heat of the day.

A number of African countries have land that extends into this vast desert, including Algeria, Chad, Egypt, Libya, Mali, Mauritania, Morocco, Niger, Sudan, and Tunisia.

The Kalahari Desert

Far to the south of the Sahara, on the other side of the equator, lionesses rest near a watering hole. The animals are in a **game reserve** in the center of the Kalahari Desert. Unlike the scorched earth of the Sahara, the Kalahari has a rich assortment of plants and wildlife. Because of this, it is sometimes referred to as a "thirstland" rather than as a desert.

The Kalahari is a large **basin** in the central part of southern Africa. It covers an area almost as large as the state of Texas. As in other deserts, rain is scarce

Vocabulary

game reserve, n. an area set aside by the government where animals are protected from hunters

basin, n. an area of land that is lower than the land around it

here and does not fall in predictable patterns. Most of the Kalahari averages about five inches of rain per year. Yet some parts get more than fifteen inches. This is usually enough moisture to support a variety of wildlife—large animals such as wildebeests, lions, antelopes, jackals, elephants, giraffes, and zebras, as well as many small animals, birds, and reptiles. Over thousands of years, one group of people called the San (or Bushmen) learned to adapt remarkably well to the dry conditions of the Kalahari.

The San People

The San learned how to find and save water. They use ostrich eggs as storage containers. Ostrich eggs are the largest eggs laid by any bird. One ostrich egg can hold as much liquid as two dozen chicken eggs. The San make a hole at each end of an ostrich egg. Then they blow out the insides, which they use for food. After a rain, they fill the hollow eggshells with water and tightly plug the two ends. Then they bury the filled shells in the sand along their routes. When the droughts come, as they always do, the San have a water supply.

The San, or Bushmen, are experts when it comes to living in the desert. Here you can see an ostrich egg being used to store water during a trek.

Chapter 3
Australia, a Dry Continent

Surviving in the Desert In the heart of Australia, a man walks across the reddish-orange earth dotted with **scrub brush**. The man is an Aborigine. Aborigines are a people who have lived on the Australian continent for at least forty thousand years. Thousands of years of close and careful observation of their environment have equipped Aborigines for survival on this mostly flat, mostly desert land.

The Big Question

What strategies have Aborigines adopted in order to survive the harsh conditions of desert life?

Vocabulary

scrub brush, n. small or short bushes and trees

The man stops to look at the earth. To the untrained eye, this spot is no different from any other spot on the ground. He stomps with his bare foot, raising little clouds of red dust. Lizards scurry into the scrub brush.

The man stops stomping and listens. He hears what he hoped to hear—the croaking of frogs, muffled beneath the earth. The frogs have been tricked. From their burrows under the surface, the desert frogs thought they were hearing the sound of thunder, signaling that rain would soon fall.

The desert sands of central Australia support an unusually large number of animals, including lizards, frogs, and rodents. These animals have learned how to survive there. Some desert frogs, for example, can store water in their bladders for long periods of time.

In a real rainstorm, the frogs emerge from their burrows and drink water from rain pools. They fill their bodies almost to bursting. Then they retreat to their burrows and use the water stored in their bodies until the next storm.

But the man has fooled the frogs. He uses sticks to dig in the earth. Finding a burrow, he pulls out a frog, its body bloated with water. Tilting his head back, he squeezes the frog until a stream of liquid squirts out, flowing down the man's parched throat.

The Outback

Two-thirds of Australia is arid or semiarid, with few rivers and little rain. The **interior** of the continent—called the Outback—is mostly desert. The Outback is so dry in some regions that it seems impossible that any creature could survive there.

Most of the desert land is covered with sand hills and spotted with short grasses. Sands often swirl into huge dunes. There is not much water in the Outback, but after a rain, rocky pools sometimes fill up. These pools are important sources of water. Water also collects in pools in old **riverbeds**, places the Australians call billabongs (dry streambeds that fill with water only in the rainy season). Sudden, heavy rains can briefly fill old riverbeds and lakes, but the water quickly washes down the riverbed, and the lakes dry out, leaving salt flats.

> **Vocabulary**
>
> **interior,** n. an area far from the coast in a country or continent
>
> **riverbed,** n. the ground at the bottom of a river
>
> **marsupial,** n. a type of mammal that carries its young in a pouch

This dry land supports many animals not found anywhere else. One such animal is the emu, a large flightless bird that can weigh as much as one hundred pounds. Another such animal is the kangaroo. Kangaroos are **marsupials**. Marsupials are well adapted to the desert conditions, mainly because they require less food than most other mammals. Kangaroos can survive on less food because it takes less energy to hop on their two hind legs than it takes to run on four legs.

An emu and its young search for food in the Outback.

The malu, or red kangaroo, is found in the deserts of Australia.

A Singing Map

Today, only a few Aborigines who live in the Australian interior continue the traditional way of life. However, before the Europeans came to Australia and disrupted their culture, the Aborigines proved that human beings can survive in even the most unforgiving climate.

According to Aborigine myth, the world was created during the "dreamtime," a time before time. The things of Earth were created by

This is an Australian gum, or eucalyptus, tree.

ancestral beings. These beings walked Earth singing out the name of each thing as they created it. They sang about the water holes, the gum trees, the riverbeds, the sand dunes. Everywhere they walked, they sang, leaving a trail of song behind them. Once the world was created and named, the beings disappeared into nature. The beings themselves disappeared, but their songs survived. This is the Aborigine myth of how their "songlines" came into being.

These songlines, or songs, have been passed by word of mouth from generation to generation for thousands of years. The songlines are literally maps of the land.

Aborigines were originally **nomadic** hunters and gatherers. These small groups of people wandered a territory that could be as large as a thousand square miles. By singing the songs, they could find the food and water necessary for survival. Their songlines led them to rocky pools of water a hundred miles away, to places where they could find wild plant foods in season, or to rich hunting grounds.

Vocabulary

nomadic, adj. moving around often in search of food; not settled in one place

A single Aborigine man on a "walkabout," or wandering journey, might reach the edge of the territory described in his songlines. He would then ask the group of Aborigines in the next territory to teach him their songlines. He could then safely travel long distances in the harsh desert, using the musical map of the songlines to find his way.

The songlines continue to provide Aborigines with the knowledge they need to survive in their desert lands.

Australia has been home to the Aborigines for thousands of years. Beautiful Aboriginal rock art has been found throughout Australia.

Chapter 4
Deserts of Asia

The Gobi One of the largest deserts in Asia, the Gobi, covers a great part of Mongolia and a part of northern China. Eighty million years ago, on what is now the vast, bone-dry region of the Gobi, a fight to the death took place.

The Big Question

How would you compare the Gobi Desert to the deserts of the Arabian Peninsula?

The Gobi in central Asia is one of the world's highest, driest deserts.

When Dinosaurs Walked the Earth

A protoceratops, a plant-eating dinosaur, peacefully grazed near the banks of a **salt marsh**. In the grasses covering the area, a predator lurked. It was a velociraptor, a small, but powerful, meat-eating dinosaur. Sensing that the moment was right, the velociraptor struck. Using its strong hind legs, it jumped on the back of the protoceratops.

Vocabulary

salt marsh, n. an area of coastal wetland, directly affected by the rise and fall of the tide

The plant-eating dinosaur fought back, using its hind legs, its long heavy tail, and its beak-shaped jaws. But neither animal could overcome the other. Soon both lay on the ground, gasping their last breaths. They died there together, predator and prey. Nearly eighty million years later, scientists discovered their bones in what had become the arid desert of the Gobi.

The Gobi Desert has been described as a treasure trove of dinosaur bones. Here you can see dinosaur bones found in the Gobi Desert.

Forbidding Landscape

Mountains almost completely surround the Gobi, blocking the path of rain clouds. Most of the Gobi's land is covered in rock and gravel, with few sand dunes.

The Gobi receives less than eight inches of rainfall per year on average. In some places, it receives less than four inches. There are rivers that come into the Gobi out of the mountains that ring the desert, but they dry up before reaching the interior.

The dryness and salty soil limit the growth of vegetation to scrub brush and grasses. Near a rare river, or where groundwater creates an oasis, poplar trees, flowering shrubs, and reeds grow.

Temperatures are extreme in the Gobi. In the winter, it can get as cold as -40°F. In the summer, temperatures can rise to more than 100°F. Extreme dryness and extreme temperatures make the Gobi one of the most forbidding of Earth's deserts.

Nomadic people of Mongolia live in the Gobi Desert.

The Arabian Peninsula

The Arabian **Peninsula** lies between the Red Sea and the Persian Gulf. Its northernmost end connects the continents of Africa and Asia. The Arabian Peninsula is made up of the countries of Yemen, Oman, Qatar, Bahrain, Kuwait, Saudi Arabia, the United Arab Emirates, and parts of Jordan and Iraq.

Parts of the peninsula are covered with rock and gravel, but most of it is a vast expanse of sand. It is the largest sand desert in the world. Sand dunes can reach as high as eight hundred feet and stretch for thirty miles. The land is mostly empty. One large part of the peninsula is called *Rub' al Khali*, meaning Empty Quarter in Arabic. The few camel-herding **Bedouin** tribes that roam this land call the region *ar-Ramlah*, or the Sand. In the summer, the average daytime temperature in the sand deserts can reach 110°F.

Vocabulary

peninsula, n. a piece of land sticking out into a body of water, so that it is almost surrounded by water

Bedouin, adj. relating to nomadic Arab tribes of Arabia and North Africa

The sand dunes of the Arabian Peninsula can be hundreds of feet high and many miles long.

Not a single significant permanent river runs through this peninsula. Most of the land is bone-dry. Where there is enough moisture for people to live, the most important plant is the date palm tree. Dates are an important food for humans. In addition, fiber from the trees is used for ropes and mats, and the wood is used for building.

Vocabulary
....
fossil fuel, n. fuel, such as oil, natural gas, and coal formed in the earth from the remains of living things

Most of the land on the peninsula belongs to Saudi Arabia. When the Saudi Arabian king, Ibn Saud, inherited his kingdom in 1932, he did not know that beneath the sand was enough oil to make him and his family very wealthy.

In 1933, officials from the American-owned Standard Oil Company offered the king 35,000 gold coins, plus a percentage of profits from anything found, for the right to drill for oil in his kingdom. After several years of preparation and drilling, more oil was discovered than anyone had imagined. Today, more than one-third of Earth's known gas and oil lies beneath the desert sands of the Arabian Peninsula. The discovery of oil in the Arabian Peninsula has made some countries there very rich.

Here you can see an oil refinery on the Arabian Peninsula. Most scientists believe that oil is formed from the remains of buried dead life forms—which is why it is called a **fossil fuel**.

Chapter 5
Deserts of North America

Mojave Desert The hottest, driest, and lowest desert in the United States is the Mojave (/mo*hah*vee/) Desert. It is located mainly in southeastern California and southern Nevada. It is one of three hot deserts running along the western side of North America.

The Big Question

If you had to survive in a desert for several days, what would you need?

Bordered by mountains on the east and west, the Mojave Desert has two rivers that wind their way through the region and dry out into salt flats. Water flowing down from the mountains can create temporary lakes, but these soon evaporate in the dry heat.

Vocabulary

yucca, n. a type of plant with pointed leaves, a long stem, and white flowers that grows in dry areas

The desert basin is covered mainly with low shrubs. But as the basin slopes upward to the mountains, the plant most associated with the Mojave Desert appears: the Joshua tree. The Joshua tree is a type of **yucca**, a member of the lily family. It grows twenty to thirty feet high and serves as home or lookout post for many species of birds, such as the ladder-backed woodpecker, the screech owl, and the sparrow hawk.

The Joshua tree of the Mojave Desert is a spiked-leaf evergreen. It does not grow anywhere else in the world.

The most famous region of the Mojave Desert is Death Valley in California. It is a low spot in the desert 130 miles long and ranging from 6 to 14 miles wide. Death Valley is both the lowest and the hottest place in the United States. It was formed when a block of earth dropped down between two **fault lines**. At 282 feet below **sea level**, Death Valley has the lowest elevation in the Western **Hemisphere**. It is also the driest place in the United States, receiving less than two inches of rain per year. As you have discovered, Death Valley boasts the all-time recognized record high temperature of 134°F.

Death Valley was once a busy area. In the 1800s, workers mined borax there, a mineral salt with many industrial uses. Covered wagons carried workers and resources in and out of the desert. Today, Death Valley is a national park.

The Sonoran Desert

In the 1800s, if you were a settler or a gold hunter traveling the southern route to California, you would have crossed the Sonoran Desert in Arizona. The trail across the desert was a two-hundred-mile stretch that earned the name Devil's Highway.

Why such a grim name? This area of bleak desert land through which the Devil's Highway passed has only one dependable water source. Coyotes, wild burros, and Gila monsters roam this dusty landscape. In some places, it is crusted with black **lava rock**. Travelers in the 1800s could not avoid seeing makeshift crosses dotting the trail, grave markers of the many travelers who died along the way.

In 1905, W. J. McGee, an editor for the National Geographic Society, set up a research station to study the plants and animals of the region. His station was located in one of the places in the desert that had water. He later wrote of his

> **Vocabulary**
>
> **fault line,** n. a crack or split in Earth's crust along which movement takes place
>
> **sea level,** n. land that is the same elevation as the surface of the sea or ocean
>
> **hemisphere,** n. either of two halves of Earth
>
> **lava rock,** n. rock formed by magma, or melted rock, that has reached Earth's surface and cooled

The Sonoran Desert stretches across Arizona and California, as well as northwestern Mexico.

encounter with two travelers who had miraculously survived this part of the desert. McGee first met gold prospectors Pablo Valencia and his partner as they passed along the trail. He invited them to spend the night at his camp. McGee described Valencia as having a "remarkably fine and vigorous physique."

Eight days later, McGee was awakened in the early morning by a piercing, agonized scream. In a nearby canyon, McGee and his assistant discovered Pablo Valencia. McGee was shocked. In just eight days, Valencia's body had shrunk until his "ribs ridged out like those of a starving horse. . . . His joints and bones stood out and the skin clung to them in a way suggesting shrunken rawhide." They poured water over Valencia's body and down his throat, but Valencia could not talk or even swallow.

Valencia had been separated from his partner, who was with the horses and supplies. He was left in the desert with only one canteen of water. He had wandered in circles through the desert, lost and disoriented from thirst. By the seventh day, he had lost forty pounds; he could not focus his eyes. He lay down in a gully, convinced that he was going to die there. But he let out one last howl, the cry that brought McGee to his rescue.

Not all of the Sonoran Desert is as harsh as the area described in this tale. In the eastern part of the desert, annual rainfall can certainly reach up to ten inches. However, the western part of the desert might only receive two inches of rain in an entire year.

The Sonoran Desert is also home to various plants, including the ocotillo (/oh*kuh*tee*yo/), or candelabra, cactus and the prickly pear cactus, as well as animals, such as the Mexican grey wolf, the mountain lion, and the great horned owl.

From left to right above are the prickly pear cactus, the ocotillo cactus, and the saguaro cactus. The image below is of the great horned owl. All live in the Sonoran Desert.

The Chihuahuan Desert

To the south and east of the Sonoran Desert lies the Chihuahuan (/chuh*wah*wahn/) Desert. Most of this desert sits on a plateau in Mexico, between two mountain ranges. It also stretches into New Mexico and West Texas. This desert has few sand dunes. The most notable are the white sand dunes at White Sands National Monument in New Mexico. The area is so isolated that the U.S. military uses part of White Sands as a testing range for bombs and missiles.

The desert plateau in Mexico receives varying amounts of rainfall, depending on elevation. Rain comes mainly in the form of brief, violent thunderstorms. Average rainfall is only about eight inches a year, although the higher elevations may receive more. Temperatures vary according to elevation, but most of the desert has cool to cold winters and hot summers.

White Sands National Park, New Mexico

Chapter 6
Deserts of South America

A Place to Hide In the late 1800s, two American outlaws named Butch Cassidy and the Sundance Kid needed a place to hide. The two men hopped a boat to South America and found the perfect place to hide out: the vast plains and desert of southern Argentina called Patagonia.

The Big Question

What are the key features of the Patagonia Desert and the Atacama Desert?

A large part of Patagonia is semiarid and treeless.

They set up a cattle ranch for a few years on the plains of Patagonia, which reminded them of the U.S. states of Wyoming and Montana. But the two outlaws never could settle down. After a few years in Patagonia, they wandered north and were killed in a shootout with soldiers in Bolivia.

Patagonia's plains and desert are in the southern part of Argentina. This area of land is bordered on the west by the soaring Andes Mountains and on the east by the Atlantic Ocean. Cliffs line almost the entire length of its coast. In the south, the cliffs can be as high as 150 feet.

Patagonia's northern border is the Rio Colorado. From there, the region stretches south 1,200 miles to the island of Tierra del Fuego (/tee*air*uh/del/ fway*goh/) at the tip of South America.

Patagonia

Much of Patagonia is a semiarid area of desert. Cattle and sheep graze on short grasses and shrubs. Rainfall averages between four and eight inches a year, but the dry winds evaporate most of the moisture, so that the entire region is almost completely without trees. Rivers flow down from the Andes toward the ocean, cutting deep canyons on the **tableland**. However, as these rivers cross the dry region, they gradually become smaller and smaller. Only a few of them make it all the way to the Atlantic.

The surface of the land is made up of gravel, rock, and, in some places, **basalt**—a result of old volcanoes in the region. The basalt flats often have hollows that contain shallow lakes.

Patagonia is in the Southern Hemisphere, so the winter months are June through September. The coldest month is July, when temperatures can drop well below freezing. Summer temperatures can climb to 100°F or more. The wind blows

Vocabulary

tableland, n. a wide, flat area of land, often higher than surrounding land; a plateau

basalt, n. a dark gray or black volcanic rock that looks like glass

The Patagonia Desert, with its short grasses and shrubs, is suitable for grazing animals.

constantly in Patagonia, down from the Andes Mountains eastward toward the Atlantic Ocean.

Big Feet, the Guanaco, and the Rhea

In 1520, Ferdinand Magellan's expedition to sail around the world stopped on the shores of what is now Argentina. According to legend, the man who recorded the events of the expedition saw huge footprints in the snow. He called the people who made those prints *Patagones* (/pat*ah*gohn*es/), Spanish for big feet. The land thus earned the name *Patagonia*. The people who made the footprints in the snow were the Tehuelche (/teh*whel*chay/) people. Stories spread throughout Europe of a gigantic race of incredibly strong people who lived in what is now Patagonia. The truth is that the Tehuelche wore very large boots stuffed with straw to keep their feet warm. This accounted for their large footprints. They were generally tall and strong but hardly the giants that the Europeans imagined them to be.

When the Spanish came to Patagonia in the 1600s, they brought horses with them. As happened in North America, horses escaped and were captured, tamed, and bred by the indigenous people. Not much is known about the Tehuelche before the horse was introduced. But with the horse, the Tehuelche took to the flat, semiarid land of Patagonia, living much like Native Americans of the Great Plains of North America. But the Tehuelche did not hunt buffalo. They hunted guanaco and rhea.

The guanaco (gwah*nah*koh/), which is related to the camel, looks like a small camel without a hump. It is about four feet tall at the shoulder, with long legs and reddish brown hair. The Tehuelche hunted guanaco on horseback, using bows and arrows and a weapon called a bola. A bola is made from two or three strands of rope with a weight tied at each end. The Tehuelche threw their bolas at the legs of animals, causing them to fall when their legs became entangled. The Tehuelche also hunted rhea, a flightless bird similar to the ostrich. The rhea is about five feet tall and weighs about fifty pounds.

The guanaco, an animal related to the camel, is found in Patagonia.

The Tehuelche hunted rhea on the plains of Patagonia.

An Argentinian cowboy demonstrates the use of bolas to capture animals.

The Atacama Desert

The Atacama Desert is located on the western coast of South America between the Pacific Ocean and the Andes. It stretches six hundred miles from southern Peru into northern Chile.

Climatologists consider parts of the Atacama Desert in Chile to be the driest place on Earth. Years can pass there without a single drop of rain. The Atacama Desert is also considered to be the oldest desert on Earth.

Other than some cacti and hardy grasses, little grows in the Atacama Desert. It is a vast desert of largely stony landscapes, salt lakes, canyons, lava rock, and even dunes. Incredibly, because of its unique **terrain**, NASA has used it to test fact-

Vocabulary

terrain, n. the landforms of a piece of land

finding equipment that could be sent to Mars. Scientists and photographers frequent this almost alien landscape.

Stargazers go there too. The Atacama Desert has incredibly clear skies at night. As a result, the Atacama Desert contains three international **observatories** that have been set up to conduct important work in the field of astronomy.

Vocabulary

observatory, n. a building from which scientists watch and study the sky

People do live on the edge of the Atacama Desert. In fact, more than a million people live in its coastal cities and towns. Iquique, Chile, is a large, thriving port city on the edge of this spectacular desert land.

This unique terrain draws scientists and photographers to the Atacama Desert.

The night sky is an extraordinary sight in the Atacama Desert.

Glossary

B

basalt, n. a dark gray or black volcanic rock that looks like glass **(38)**

basin, n. an area of land that is lower than the land around it **(16)**

Bedouin, adj. relating to nomadic Arab tribes of Arabia and North Africa **(28)**

C

climatologist, n. a scientist who studies weather patterns over time **(4)**

D

desertification, n. natural or human processes that turn fertile land into a desert **(10)**

E

evaporation, n. the process by which a liquid changes to a vapor or gas **(4)**

F

fault line, n. a crack or split in Earth's crust along which movement takes place **(32)**

fossil fuel, n. fuel, such as oil, natural gas, and coal formed in the earth from the remains of living things **(29)**

G

game reserve, n. an area set aside by the government where animals are protected from hunters **(16)**

H

hemisphere, n. either of two halves of Earth **(32)**

I

interior, n. an area far from the coast in a country or continent **(20)**

L

lava rock, n. rock formed by magma, or melted rock, that has reached Earth's surface and cooled **(32)**

M

marsupial, n. a type of mammal that carries its young in a pouch **(20)**

N

nomadic, adj. moving around often in search of food; not settled in one place **(23)**

O

oasis, n. an area in the desert where there are plants and water **(14)**

observatory, n. a building from which scientists watch and study the sky **(42)**

P

peninsula, n. a piece of land sticking out into a body of water, so that it is almost surrounded by water **(28)**

polar, adj. relating to a geographic pole or the area around it **(2)**

precipitation, n. water falling to Earth's surface as rain, hail, snow, or sleet **(4)**

R

radiate, v. to send out **(15)**

riverbed, n. the ground at the bottom of a river **(20)**

S

salt flat, n. an area of land where evaporation has left a layer of salt **(15)**

salt marsh, n. an area of coastal wetland, directly affected by the rise and fall of the tide **(26)**

scrub brush, n. small or short bushes and trees (18)

sea level, n. land that is the same elevation as the surface of the sea or ocean (32)

semiarid, adj. describing locations with little precipitation, but with enough moisture to support the growth of grasses, shrubs, and a few scattered trees (10)

T

tableland, n. a wide, flat area of land, often higher than surrounding land; a plateau (38)

terrain, n. the landforms of a piece of land (41)

Y

yucca, n. a type of plant with pointed leaves, a long stem, and white flowers that grows in dry areas (30)

CKHG™
Core Knowledge HISTORY AND GEOGRAPHY™

Series Editor-In-Chief
E.D. Hirsch, Jr.

Editorial Directors
Linda Bevilacqua and Rosie McCormick

Subject Matter Expert

Charles F. Gritzner, PhD

Distinguished Professor Emeritus of Geography, South Dakota State University

Illustration and Photo Credits

© NHPA/Photoshot/Photoshot/SuperStock: 21

agf photo/SuperStock: 14

Andy Selinger/age fotostock/SuperStock : 9

Art Wolfe Stock/Cultura Limited/SuperStock: Cover C, 39

Charles O. Cecil/age fotostock/SuperStock: 29

CHARTON Franck/Hemis.fr/SuperStock: 16, 17

D. Parer & E. Parer-Cook/Pantheon/SuperStock: Cover B, 19

Dennis Mook/SuperStock: 34

Edwin Remsberg/age fotostock/SuperStock: 28

FLPA/SuperStock: 21

Imagemore/SuperStock: 11

Ingram Publishing/SuperStock: 7

Juniors/SuperStock: 41

K.D. McGraw/Rainbow/SuperStock: i, iii, 7

LOOK-foto/SuperStock: 15

M. Watson/ardea.com/Pantheo/Pantheon/SuperStock: 36–37

Mark Newman/SuperStock: 34

Mint Images/SuperStock: 40

Newman Mark/Prisma/SuperStock : 34

Paul Mayall/imageBROKER/SuperStock : 22

Pete Oxford/Minden Pictures/SuperStock : 24–25

Philippe Michel/age fotostock/SuperStock : 1, 27

Photononstop/SuperStock: 8

PITAMITZ Sergio/Hemis.fr/SuperStock: 43

Prisma/SuperStock: 4

Radomir Hofman/age fotostock/SuperStock: 33

RIEGER Bertrand/Hemis.fr/SuperStock: 41

robertharding/SuperStock: Cover D, 12–13

Seth Resnick/SuperStock: 42–43

Stock Connection/SuperStock: 26

Susan E. Degginger/age fotostock/SuperStock: 35

Tom Vezo/Minden Pictures/SuperStock: 34

Universal Images Group/SuperStock: 23

Westend61/SuperStock: 2–3

Yva Momatiuk & John Eastcott/Minden Pictures/SuperStock: Cover A, 30–31